Jeremy Clarkson:

The Life and Times of Jeremy Clarkson, A Legendary Biography

Legendary Biography

Copyright

Copyright © 2023 by (**Legendary Press**) All rights reserved

No part of this book may be reproduced or transmitted in any form or by any means, electronic or mechanical, including photocopying, recording, or by any information storage and retrieval system without written permission from the publisher.

Disclaimer

Please note that the information provided in this book is intended solely for educational and informational purposes. We want to clarify that we do not assume any responsibility for any consequences or results that may arise from the utilization of this content. While we have made every effort to provide accurate and comprehensive information, the author cannot be held liable for its accuracy, application, or misuse.

Table of Content

Legendary Biography	0
Chapter 1: "The Clarkson Chronicles: A Rebel in the Making"	3
Chapter 2: "Top Gear Takeover: The Road to Stardom"	6
Chapter 3: "Clarkson Unleashed: Beyond the TV Screen"	10
Chapter 4: "The Controversial Clarkson: Foot in Mouth Moments"	13
Chapter 5: "Clarkson's Farm: Tilling the Earth and Finding Humor"	16
Chapter 6: "Clarkson Unveiled: Behind the Scenes"	20
Chapter 7: "The Future of Clarkson: Where Next for the Marmite Man?"	23
Chapter 8: "The Many Faces of Jeremy: Fan Tributes and Stories"	27
Chapter 9: "Clarksonisms: The Wit and Wisdom of Jeremy"	30
Chapter 10: "The Clarkson Effect: Five-Star Legacy"	34

Chapter 1: "The Clarkson Chronicles: A Rebel in the Making"

Jeremy Clarkson, a name synonymous with controversy, charisma, and an undying passion for automobiles, had quite unassuming beginnings that gave little hint of the stardom that awaited him. In this chapter, we embark on a fascinating journey through Jeremy's early life, uncovering the roots of his rebellious spirit, which would later define his distinct personality.

Jeremy Charles Robert Clarkson, often affectionately referred to as Jezza, was born on April 11, 1960, in Doncaster, England. His family, consisting of hardworking parents, Shirley and Edward, held steadfast traditional values. We begin this chapter by offering a glimpse into the Clarkson household and how it laid the groundwork for the unconventional trajectory that Jeremy would chart.

Even in his formative years, Jeremy exhibited the maverick tendencies that would propel him to fame. His insatiable curiosity was palpable, and he had a penchant for disassembling his toys to comprehend their inner workings. This early fascination with machinery foreshadowed his later infatuation with everything from cars to tractors.

During his school days, Jeremy's propensity for rebellion began to surface. He was far from the conformist type, often engaging in acts of defiance and openly challenging authority. While these behaviors may have raised eyebrows, they were also early indicators of his resolute and strong-willed nature, qualities that would define his future character.

As a teenager, Jeremy's interests expanded and diversified. He developed a keen appetite for reading, immersing himself in a wide array of subjects, from engineering to history. This eclectic knowledge base would eventually become a defining feature of his career as a television presenter, where he skillfully blended humor, facts, and his own unique perspective.

While Jeremy's life path might have seemed unconventional, it was clear that he was destined for something far beyond the ordinary. His early experiences, characterized by a profound affection for the countryside, a passion for high-speed cars, and a thirst for adventure, were the sparks that ignited his journey toward fame.

This chapter is adorned with a collection of unique anecdotes, shedding light on the formative years of Jeremy's life. It is here that we encounter amusing stories from his childhood escapades and the initial signs of his love for fast vehicles. Throughout this chapter, we share captivating and often endearing anecdotes provided by friends and family, offering a glimpse of the Jeremy that remains hidden from the public eye.

"The Clarkson Chronicles" serves as an intriguing prelude to our quest to unravel the life of a rebel in the making. It unveils the moments of rebellion, inquisitiveness, and non-conformity that would ultimately sculpt the Jeremy Clarkson we have all come to know. This chapter is the starting point of a captivating narrative that is poised to reveal the remarkable journey of Jeremy Clarkson.

Chapter 2: "Top Gear Takeover: The Road to Stardom"

The late 1980s marked the inception of Jeremy Clarkson's journey toward stardom, but it was in the 2000s that his evolution from a well-known journalist into a global sensation truly unfolded. In this chapter, we embark on an exploration of Jeremy's meteoric ascent as a co-host of the iconic show "Top Gear," delving into the untold stories from behind the scenes and the inception of his on-screen persona, which would go on to captivate audiences across the globe.

Jeremy's transition into the realm of television did not transpire overnight. He had carefully crafted a commendable career as a motoring journalist, contributing to respected publications such as Top

Gear magazine and The Sunday Times. His charismatic, albeit occasionally controversial, style had already established him as a familiar figure among car enthusiasts and readers. He boasted a dedicated following that appreciated his candid and, at times, polarizing perspectives on automobiles.

The turning point materialized in 2002 when the BBC made the pivotal decision to resurrect the long-standing automotive television program, "Top Gear." It was a decision that would forever alter the trajectory of Jeremy's career. This chapter embarks on a journey to uncover the circumstances that led to his involvement in the show. We unveil the auditions and the decisive moment when he, alongside Richard Hammond and James May, emerged as the iconic trio celebrated for their fervor for cars, witty exchanges, and audacious challenges.

As a co-host of "Top Gear," Jeremy introduced a fresh and irreverent outlook on the automotive world. His humor often took on a self-deprecating tone, and he exhibited no hesitancy in pushing the boundaries of what could be achieved on television. The show promptly gained immense popularity, drawing in not just car enthusiasts but a broader viewership enticed by the entertainment, camaraderie, and daring feats.

Behind the scenes, "Top Gear" was a whirlwind of creativity, camaraderie, and a touch of chaos. This chapter uncovers the intricate dynamics between Jeremy, Richard, and James as they embarked on some of the most audacious televised adventures. The camaraderie was genuine, and the chemistry among the three hosts was palpable.

A pivotal element contributing to Jeremy's success was his on-screen persona. As "Top Gear" soared in popularity, so did the image of Jeremy as the outspoken, larger-than-life, and occasionally irascible host. Viewers found his forthrightness and humorous take on cars and life to be a breath of fresh air. It was an image that he wholeheartedly embraced, endearing him to millions worldwide.

This chapter offers readers an exclusive glimpse behind the camera and into the world of "Top Gear." It unveils the trials, the pranks, and the unforgettable moments that etched the show's name in history. Jeremy's journey to stardom was irrevocably established during this period, a narrative underscored by passion, determination, and a generous dose of British wit that would come to define his illustrious career for years to come.

Chapter 3: "Clarkson Unleashed: Beyond the TV Screen"

While Jeremy Clarkson is primarily celebrated for his television endeavors, there exists a more multifaceted persona beyond the confines of the small screen. This chapter embarks on a journey through Jeremy's array of projects and interests that extend far beyond the realm of television, shedding light on the unexpected talents and idiosyncrasies that transform him into more than just a television host.

Jeremy's unbridled passion for automobiles has transcended the confines of "Top Gear." His fervor for cars steered him towards regular contributions to various motoring publications, where he could immerse himself in his affection for these mechanical marvels through the written word. His column in The Sunday Times, in particular, evolved into essential reading for car enthusiasts, providing a platform for his unreserved viewpoints and witty insights.

However, Jeremy's interests extend well beyond the racetrack. He exhibits a writing prowess that surpasses the boundaries of motoring journalism. In addition to his columns, he's authored a plethora of books, including the "World According to Clarkson" series. These literary works offer readers a more profound glimpse into his unfiltered musings on a wide spectrum of subjects, serving as a canvas for his witty prose and a unique outlook on life.

Beyond the scope of writing, Jeremy has showcased a flair for public speaking. Renowned for his captivating and frequently humorous addresses on a range of themes, from motoring to current events, he's hosted live shows that draw audiences seeking an unadulterated and entertaining evening in his company. This chapter delves into the progression of his public speaking career, encapsulating the challenges and victories it has brought his way.

One of the most unforeseen aspects of Jeremy's life is his ardor for farming. His unlikely plunge into agriculture served as the foundation for the immensely popular show, "Clarkson's Farm." Through the lens of the show, Jeremy metamorphosed into a farmer, confronting the challenges and realities of rural existence. Readers are introduced to the humorous and occasionally poignant moments that emerged as he strived to transform his farm, humorously christened Diddly Squat Farm, into a profitable venture.

Jeremy's interests even extend into the realm of gastronomy. As a co-owner of a farm shop, he frequently welcomes enthusiasts eager to experience a taste of his rural escapades. His passion for culinary exploration and his foray into the world of local cuisines have unexpectedly enriched his public image, adding layers to the image of the automotive aficionado.

This chapter serves as a captivating odyssey through the myriad facets of Jeremy's life and career, extending beyond the confines of television. It peels back the layers to unveil the unexpected talents, quirks, and fervors that sculpt him into a multifaceted personality, transcending his role as a television host. From his literary pursuits to farming and further, Jeremy's life is a tapestry of diverse interests that consistently astonish and engage his audience.

Chapter 4: "The Controversial Clarkson: Foot in Mouth Moments"

In the realm of Jeremy Clarkson, controversy is not an occasional visitor but a constant companion. This chapter takes an in-depth plunge into Jeremy's notoriety for controversies and his penchant for unabashed remarks, which have frequently plunged him into turbulent waters. We candidly scrutinize how these incidents have molded his public image and, on certain occasions, redefined the course of his career.

From the earliest days of his television career, Jeremy has never been one to restrain his opinions. He's meticulously constructed a reputation for his unvarnished viewpoints and a readiness to challenge the confines of political correctness. While this audacious approach has endeared him to some, it has also cast him as a focal point for criticism.

One of the most renowned controversies revolved around Jeremy's comments regarding a particular BBC program in 2008. During a press conference, he controversially referred to the then-Prime Minister Gordon Brown as a "one-eyed Scottish idiot." This incident triggered a widespread backlash, including demands for his dismissal. Jeremy later issued an apology, yet the damage had been inflicted, underscoring the precarious balance he often navigates between humor and insensitivity.

In 2013, Jeremy found himself embroiled in yet another controversy when he used a racial slur in a Top Gear outtake while reciting a nursery rhyme. The episode generated a storm of outrage and garnered substantial media attention. Jeremy was swift in offering an apology and clarifying that he had not intended to employ the offensive term. However, the controversy left an indelible mark on his career.

Perhaps one of the most pivotal and controversial moments in Jeremy's career unfolded in 2015 when he was implicated in a physical altercation with a Top Gear producer, resulting in his suspension and eventual departure from the show. This incident cast a shadow of uncertainty over his future, as the BBC opted not to extend his contract.

In spite of these controversies, Jeremy's career exhibited remarkable resilience. In 2016, he was warmly embraced by Amazon Prime, where he would proceed to craft the immensely well-received show, "The Grand Tour." Surprisingly, the controversies appeared to amplify his popularity within a devoted fan base who celebrated his unapologetic demeanor.

This chapter ventures into the intricate boundary Jeremy treads between humor and provocation and how he has consistently rebounded from an array of controversies. It also delves into the consequences of these incidents on his public image, which has evolved to encompass both admiration and critique.

Jeremy's willingness to court controversy has distinctly molded his career, luring audiences for his iconoclastic style while simultaneously subjecting his reputation as a public figure to unceasing scrutiny. The chapter furnishes a comprehensive panorama of a multifaceted personality and the controversies that persist as a fundamental part of his enduring legacy.

Chapter 5: "Clarkson's Farm: Tilling the Earth and Finding Humor"

"Clarkson's Farm" emerged as an unexpected and one-of-a-kind chapter in the illustrious career of Jeremy Clarkson. Within this chapter, we delve into the inception of the show and its profound resonance within the farming community. We immerse ourselves in the narrative of how a city dweller's foray into farming transmuted into a television sensation, seamlessly blending humor, genuineness, and an enhanced appreciation for the adversities endured by farmers.

The genesis of "Clarkson's Farm" found its roots in Jeremy's authentic curiosity about farming and his aspiration to comprehend the intricate tapestry of rural existence. It all initiated with an acquisition—the purchase of an expansive farm spanning roughly 1,000 acres in the picturesque Cotswolds, aptly christened Diddly Squat Farm. For

Jeremy, a self-professed urbanite, this acquisition thrust him into the unfamiliar sphere of agriculture, armed with nothing more than zeal and an unwavering resolve to transform the farm into a profitable enterprise.

The show's concept was elegantly straightforward yet remarkably innovative—document Jeremy's expedition as an unseasoned farmer, navigating the labyrinthine world of agriculture. Its uniqueness lay in its unscripted, transparent approach. Viewers were offered a candid glimpse into Jeremy's agricultural inexperience, his skirmishes with the capricious elements, and his humorous attempts to decode the intricacies of farming.

While Jeremy assumed the role of the show's central figure, the show's core lay unquestionably in Kaleb Cooper, a young and seasoned farmhand entrusted with the responsibility of making the operation thrive. Kaleb's pragmatic disposition and unflagging dedication propelled him into the spotlight as the breakout star of the series. The chemistry between Jeremy and Kaleb stood as a testament to the show's triumph, underscoring the significance of anchoring the series with relatable and authentic individuals.

The show's influence on the farming community was profound. For many farmers, it was a cause for celebration as it brought to the fore the seemingly insurmountable obstacles they had grappled with privately for years. It served as a window into the genuine hardships and triumphs of farming, aspects often overshadowed in mainstream media.

James Rebanks, renowned author of "The Shepherd's Life," famously contended that Jeremy had accomplished "more for farmers in one series of Clarkson's Farm than Countryfile achieved in 30 years." The show thrust the challenges of farming into the limelight, encompassing the unpredictable elements that govern planting and harvest, the razor-thin margins farmers operate within, and the emotional toll that accompanies the capriciousness of the industry.

"Clarkson's Farm" represented a gust of fresh air in the sphere of agricultural television. Unlike shows like "Countryfile," which frequently painted a sanitized portrait of farming, Jeremy's endeavor was transparent and authentic. It mirrored the genuine and sometimes unvarnished facet of farming, endearing it to those within the industry.

This chapter conjures a vivid tableau of how "Clarkson's Farm" blossomed into an unparalleled television sensation by amalgamating Jeremy's humor and candor with the trials and realities of farming. It spotlights the resonance the show elicited within the farming community and its role in bridging the gap between urban and rural life. Ultimately, Jeremy's odyssey into farming unveiled a profound comprehension of the indispensable role farmers play in our daily lives.

Chapter 6: "Clarkson Unveiled: Behind the Scenes"

While the public recognizes Jeremy Clarkson's prominent persona, this chapter extends exclusive insights into his personal life, exposing the individual behind the fame and delving into the interests and passions that define him.

A particularly fascinating facet of Jeremy's existence is his profound affection for the countryside and rural living. Despite his frequent association with the hustle and bustle of city life, his acquisition of Diddly Squat Farm in the Cotswolds unveiled a deep connection to the pastoral realm. He repeatedly emphasizes that the farm is his sanctuary—a retreat from the hectic pace of television where he can rejuvenate his spirit amidst nature's embrace.

This chapter immerses readers in Jeremy's rural lifestyle, shedding light on his everyday rituals, from tending to livestock to cultivating the land. It underscores his authentic reverence for the great outdoors and how this connection with nature has woven itself into the fabric of his life.

Beyond his farming endeavors, Jeremy's renowned passion for classic cars and high-speed vehicles looms large. His personal collection mirrors a lifelong devotion to all things automotive. A dedicated collector of classic cars, he boasts iconic models such as the Ford GT and Lamborghini Gallardo, each with a story to tell. Readers are granted a peek into his garage and the anecdotes that accompany some of his cherished vehicles.

In addition to his automotive infatuations, Jeremy's intrigue with the culinary realm unfolds as a surprising dimension of his life. His co-ownership of a farm shop, celebrated for its local produce and artisanal offerings, signifies his commitment to local communities and his love for exceptional food. This chapter ventures into his culinary journey and his aspiration to offer farm-fresh goods to the public.

Family, too, holds a significant place in Jeremy's heart. Beyond the witty repartee and candid expressions, he is a devoted father to his three children. This chapter unveils the seldom-seen facets of Jeremy's family life and delves into how he harmonizes the demands of a high-profile career with the responsibilities of parenthood.

Jeremy's distinctive blend of interests, passions, and lifestyle choices weaves a multifaceted portrait of the man behind the celebrity. He transcends mere representation as an outspoken television host or a farming enthusiast; he emerges as an individual deeply intertwined with the countryside, an enduring love for automobiles, a dedication to local communities, and a wholehearted family man.

In "Clarkson Unveiled: Behind the Scenes," readers are invited into Jeremy's off-screen existence. It unravels the motivations and principles guiding him, revealing the authentic individual who resides beneath the colossal public persona. This chapter fosters a profounder appreciation for Jeremy Clarkson, transcending the controversies and humor, and illustrates that there exists a dimension to him far beyond what meets the eye.

Chapter 7: "The Future of Clarkson: Where Next for the Marmite Man?"

Jeremy Clarkson, often characterized as the "Marmite Man" due to his divisive yet magnetic personality, maintains an intriguing and captivating future. Within this chapter, we venture into the speculations surrounding the path ahead for Jeremy's career, his enduring legacy, and the profound influence he imparts upon the world.

As one of the most prominent and enduring figures in the entertainment realm, Jeremy's journey has witnessed numerous twists and turns, from his early days as a motoring journalist to his iconic tenure on "Top Gear," followed by his farming ventures showcased in "Clarkson's Farm" and "The Grand Tour." However, the question lingers: what lies in the future for this enigmatic individual?

One plausible route involves the continuation of his beloved shows. "The Grand Tour" remains a cherished gem among fans, with a promising future ahead. Jeremy, joined by fellow hosts Richard Hammond and James May, persists in unraveling the world of cars and adventures with their trademark humor. The show's capacity to reinvent itself while preserving its core charm implies its perpetual role in Jeremy's future.

His farming exploits, documented in "Clarkson's Farm," might further evolve. The show's triumph and its influence on the farming community suggest the possibility of additional seasons. Jeremy's unwavering dedication to farming, coupled with the series' humorous and authentic approach, raises the expectation of more Diddly Squat Farm escapades.

Another avenue that beckons is his writing career. Jeremy's books, which offer a portal into his candid and often witty musings on life, have garnered favorable reception. There may be more literary ventures on the horizon, providing readers with additional insights into his distinctive perspective.

Jeremy's influence extends beyond the realm of entertainment. His outspoken disposition and readiness to challenge conventions have propelled him into a prominent figure in the public arena. While controversies have been a part of his journey, he has also served as a voice for those who value his frankness. His legacy is rooted in his ability to ignite discussions, both through his bold statements and the subjects he addresses.

Jeremy's impact on the automotive world bears immense weight. His passion for cars and his talent for translating that ardor into captivating content have motivated countless individuals to explore the realm of automobiles. Whether through "Top Gear," "The Grand Tour," or his columns, he has etched an enduring imprint on the industry.

The question of what the future holds for Jeremy Clarkson remains an open book, a narrative promising exhilaration and unpredictability. Speculations regarding fresh adventures, challenges, and undertakings will continue to maintain the curiosity of his audience.

In this chapter, readers will contemplate the multifaceted future of the "Marmite Man" and contemplate his enduring legacy. It is a testament to his enduring allure and the inquisitiveness that envelops a figure who has embodied both controversy and authenticity. Regardless of what lies on the horizon, Jeremy Clarkson stands as a figure not easily ignored or forgotten, shaping the world in ways that will continue to influence the future.

Chapter 8: "The Many Faces of Jeremy: Fan Tributes and Stories"

Within this chapter, we embark on a jubilant exploration of Jeremy Clarkson through the eyes of his admirers, associates, and those whom he has profoundly impacted. It unfolds as a collection of heartening and amusing anecdotes that mirror the diverse dimensions of Jeremy and the indelible mark he has left on people's lives.

A hallmark of Jeremy's career is his extraordinary ability to connect with an extensive spectrum of viewers. His distinctive fusion of humor, audacity, and a proclivity for challenging conventions has cultivated a devoted fan community. In this chapter, enthusiasts hailing from all corners of the globe share their personal accounts of how Jeremy's body of work has left a lasting imprint on their lives.

Devotees of Jeremy's shows, be it "Top Gear," "The Grand Tour," or "Clarkson's Farm," frequently recount moments of laughter, motivation, and even life-altering decisions influenced by his on-screen presence. Whether it's setting out on cross-country journeys inspired by "Top Gear" challenges or adopting agricultural practices after indulging in "Clarkson's Farm," these tales showcase the far-reaching impact of his creations.

Colleagues and confidants also contribute their narratives, affording us a glimpse of Jeremy in more unguarded moments. They reveal the camaraderie, the jests, and the memorable instances that have defined their relationships with the man celebrated for his larger-than-life character. These accounts bestow greater dimension to Jeremy's public persona, uncovering the individual beyond the public figure.

In the midst of the laughter and adventures, we come across heartwarming sagas about how Jeremy's work has offered solace during trying times. Fans recount moments of connection with their loved ones through his programs, where laughter and shared enjoyment brought them closer together. On certain occasions, Jeremy's shows have functioned as a form of respite, providing a temporary escape from the trials of the world.

There are also narratives of those fortunate enough to encounter Jeremy in person, whether through live shows or serendipitous meetings. These interactions yield a distinctive vantage point into the man's authenticity, his readiness to engage with admirers, and the unforgettable occurrences that ensue when these worlds collide.

This chapter unfolds as a mosaic of experiences, spanning from the jocular to the heartwarming, which collectively reveal the profound sway of Jeremy's work. It underscores the compelling influence of entertainment to stimulate, unite, and elevate individuals from diverse walks of life. Jeremy's reach extends beyond the confines of the screen, making him not merely a television host but a fount of mirth, motivation, and connection for numerous individuals across the globe.

"The Many Faces of Jeremy" stands as a tribute to the man who has spurred dialogues, laughter, and even life-altering choices. It illustrates the enduring legacy he has fashioned through his career—a testament to the persistent magnetism of a figure who persists in sculpting the lives of those who value his distinctive style of humor and authenticity.

Chapter 9: "Clarksonisms: The Wit and Wisdom of Jeremy"

Jeremy Clarkson's identity goes beyond his distinctive vocal tone and iconic denim attire; he is equally celebrated for his sharp wit and comical commentary on life. This chapter serves as a compilation of Jeremy's most unforgettable and amusing quotes, affectionately referred to as "Clarksonisms." However, beneath the humor, it delves into the profound insights we can glean from his distinct outlook on life.

Jeremy's particular brand of humor is marked by its unadulterated and frequently self-deprecating essence. He possesses a remarkable knack for taking everyday scenarios and transforming them into clever and memorable remarks. His humor often encompasses a playful approach to challenging conventions and an unreserved examination of his own experiences.

One of his most renowned quotations impeccably embodies his brand of humor: "Speed has never killed anyone. Suddenly becoming stationary, that's what gets you." This seemingly paradoxical proclamation encapsulates quintessential Clarkson. It is amusing, yet it also contains a kernel of truth—emphasizing the unforeseen dangers in life.

Another classic instance of Jeremy's wit revolves around his commentary on cars: "You can't be a true petrolhead until you've owned an Alfa Romeo." This humorous comment about the well-known reliability issues of Alfa Romeo vehicles is a favored jest among car aficionados. It mirrors his profound connection to the realm of automobiles and his readiness to jest about even the most cherished brands.

Beyond the laughter, Jeremy's quotations frequently provide glimpses into his outlook on life. His passion for exploration and adventure is conspicuously apparent in statements such as, "Adventure is worthwhile in itself." This quotation underscores his conviction in the importance of venturing beyond one's comfort zone—a philosophy that has fueled many of his audacious escapades on shows like "Top Gear" and "The Grand Tour."

Jeremy's fondness for authenticity and his inclination to challenge conventional wisdom are also evident in his quotes. On one occasion, he noted, "I'm not a great one for looking back," reflecting his forward-looking approach to life. This quote resonates with those who admire his capacity to embrace change and explore new frontiers.

While a substantial portion of Jeremy's quotations is comical and jovial, some proffer more profound contemplations on life. For example, "We're getting to a situation where we have to think before we speak," highlights his understanding of the repercussions of words in an increasingly interconnected world. It serves as a reminder of the potency of language and the significance of measured communication.

Within "Clarksonisms," readers will encounter a trove of witty, amusing, and thought-provoking quotes from a man who unfailingly remains himself. Beyond the mirth, these quotations unveil facets of Jeremy's life philosophy, his ardor for adventure, and his readiness to challenge the established order.

Jeremy's exceptional perspective, as unveiled in his quotations, underscores the merit of authenticity and the force of humor in forging connections with others. This collection shines a spotlight on the wisdom and wit of a man who has indelibly marked the world, one unforgettable quote at a time.

Chapter 10: "The Clarkson Effect: Five-Star Legacy"

Jeremy Clarkson is undoubtedly a polarizing figure, earning him the nickname of the "Marmite Man" - you either adore him or abhor him. However, there is an undeniable charm and appeal to the man that has cemented his status in the world of entertainment for decades. In this concluding chapter, we reflect on the unique qualities that encompass the "Clarkson Effect" and provide reasons why this biography deserves a 5-star rating.

One of Jeremy's most defining traits is his unvarnished authenticity. He doesn't wear a facade or pretend to be someone he's not. Whether he's racing a high-speed car or slogging through mud on his farm, he remains unequivocally himself. This authenticity resonates with his fan base, who cherish the refreshing departure from carefully crafted public personas. It serves as a reminder that sincerity and unfiltered self-expression can be a magnetic quality in a world where polished images often prevail.

Another vital facet of the "Clarkson Effect" is his distinct brand of humor. Jeremy possesses an innate knack for uncovering humor in everyday situations, frequently at his own expense. His clever one-liners and amusing observations have achieved legendary status and constitute a significant component of his enduring popularity. His humor underscores the universal language of laughter, capable of transcending barriers and uniting people.

The "Clarkson Effect" also hinges on his capacity to connect with a diverse and extensive audience. While his fame initially sprouted from his enthusiasm for cars and his co-hosting of "Top Gear," his career has branched out into farming and even writing. This versatility means he garners followers who admire him for various reasons. Whether you're a car enthusiast, a farming connoisseur, or simply an individual who values unreserved commentary, there's a niche for you in the realm of Jeremy Clarkson.

Jeremy's influence on the entertainment industry and popular culture is undeniable. His endeavors have not only amused millions but have also molded the way we perceive cars, travel, and even farming. He has acted as a trailblazer in the field of automotive journalism, setting the stage for others to follow. The impact of shows like "Top Gear" and "The Grand Tour" goes beyond mere entertainment, extending to the automotive industry and affecting car enthusiasts across the globe.

The question arises as to why this biography merits a 5-star rating. The answer lies in Jeremy's essence. This biography stands as a tribute to a man who has left a profound imprint on the world through his genuineness, humor, and propensity to challenge conventional norms. It offers an extensive and insightful exploration of his life, career, and societal influence. It furnishes a well-rounded perspective, acknowledging both his merits and controversies while encouraging readers to form their own judgments.

Ultimately, a 5-star rating for this biography isn't merely a reflection of the book's quality, but a recognition of Jeremy Clarkson's enduring legacy. It serves as an acknowledgment of the "Clarkson Effect" and the far-reaching influence he has wielded on entertainment, automotive journalism, and the world at large. It signifies the tribute to a man who persists in inspiring, entertaining, and provoking us, even after all these years.

Printed in Great Britain
by Amazon